STORE DESIGNS

FOR THE '90s

STORE DESIGNS
FOR THE
'90s

nRma

The Library
of Applied
Design

PBC INTERNATIONAL, Inc.

Distributor to the book trade in the United States and Canada:

Rizzoli International Publications Inc.
300 Park Avenue South
New York, NY 10010

Distributor to the art trade in the United States:

Letraset USA
40 Eisenhower Drive
Paramus, NJ 07652

Distributor to the art trade in Canada:

Letraset Canada Limited
555 Alden Road
Markham, Ontario L3R 3L5, Canada

Distributed throughout the rest of the world:

Hearst Books International
105 Madison Avenue
New York, NY 10016

Library of Congress Cataloging-in-Publication Data

Store designs for the '90s / by the editors of PBC
 International with the National Retail Merchants
Association.

    p.   cm.
  Includes index.
  ISBN 0-86636-144-6
  1. Stores, Retail—Themes, motives. 2. Stores,
Retail—Designs and plans. 3. Stores, Retail—
Remodeling. I. PBC International. II. National Retail
Merchants Association.
NA6220.S78   1989
725' .21—dc20   89-9378
                        CIP

*CAVEAT—Information in this test is believed accurate, and
will pose no problem for the student or casual reader.
However, the authors were often constrained by information
contained in signed release forms, information that could
have been in error or not included at all. Any
misinformation (or lack of information) is the result of failure
in these attestations. The authors have done whatever is
possible to insure accuracy.*

Color separation, printing and binding by
Toppan Printing Co. (H.K.) Ltd. Hong Kong

Typography by
RMP Publication Services

10 9 8 7 6 5 4 3 2 1

CONTENTS

FOREWORD

For a number of years, NRMA has been publishing books on excellence in store interior design. The reason is simple: If it is to survive in an age of constant change, the retail enterprise must possess individuality.

The marriage of ideas with talent has given us a new generation of store designer and a new generation of store design. Hence retailers, no matter how large or small, must crete a unique atmosphere and environment.

The challenge of store interior design is constant visual stimulation. To be selected for an award in the Institute of Store Planners (ISP) and the National Retail Merchants Association (NRMA) Store Interior Design Competition, a designer or firm must create an outstanding environment that enhances and attracts the shopping public. The designer's product must never be boring or repetitive. The winning designs on these pages exceeded those standards and challenges.

Enjoy your copy of *Store Designs for the '90s*. We hope it will be a source of inspiration in your own pursuit of innovative, imaginative and productive store design.

James R. Williams, President
**National Retail Merchants
Association**

INTRODUCTION

Store interior designers have often remained unrecognized. We realize their importance, but we quite often fail to acknowledge their overall contribution to the success of the retail enterprise. *Store Designs for the '90s* is a combined effort of the National Retail Merchants Association (NRMA) and the Institute of Store Planners (ISP), and it focuses attention on those outstanding people and firms whose work has been selected to receive the ISP/NRMA Interior Design Awards. The competitions were administered by Ruth Mellengaard, ISP International Vice-President.

This book is intended to serve as an example of creative excellence in design for senior store management, visual merchandising directors, store planners and designers, architects, teachers and students. Further, store interior design is a recognized tool of marketing and an aid to selling goods and services; hence, this book should contribute to every merchant's ongoing retail education.

There is a great deal of information provided on the following pages; the ultimate use of this material is up to you. The publication of this book does not, however, constitute an express or implied endorsement, by the National Retail Merchants Association or the Institute of Store Planners, of any particular product, service or firm.

Charles A. Binder,
Executive Vice-President
National Retail Merchants Association

Newton J. Fassler, FISP, AIA;
International President
Institute of Store Planners

chapter

12345
678

NEW FULL LINE
DEPARTMENT STORE

J. W. Robinson's
Costa Mesa, California

FIRST PRIZE, New Full-Line Department Store

Designer: Hambrecht Terrell International

This is the flagship store for J. W. Robinson's, its largest in 30 years. The store was designed to be one of a kind, to be competitive and to occupy a unique niche in the marketplace. The design is distinctly "Southern California" with grand proportions—contemporary, sleek and clean; its three-levels are equivalent in height to a nine-story residential building.

The overall design is described in four words: spacious, sleek, contemporary and sophisticated. There is extensive use of natural light, glass and mirrors; bold geometric forms; and grand proportions. The interior is the epitome of luxurious space, designed to attract customers for whom shopping is enjoyable.

Drama is achieved with bold and imposing elements escalator design and its visual impact as a geometric form, plus oversized platform "stages" in departments such as Fashions and Domestics), through creative application of natural materials such as woods and marbles and by accent use of the color black throughout, including black faux marble mannequins and black fixtures. This drama tempts customers to explore all departments and niches of the store.

Natural light permeates the store through bold windows, dramatic skylights, glass displays and faceted mirror panels, lending a crystalline effect. The two massive skylights step down in three planes, allowing shoppers on every floor to view them.

Muted colors are used throughout, giving tonal depths; here the store becomes "tonal" rather than "textural." Throughout are three major materials: pale woods, cream marbles and black trim. A muted palette is an excellent backdrop for changing merchandise with the season.

Many departments are octagons along an axis, which facilitates movement and gives shoppers a visual reference. Fixtures and displays complement one another, and in many cases are integrated. In cosmetics, for example, three-dimensional layered glass is used as a visual statement.

This store is among a new breed of upscale department stores—stores with amenities, to serve customers who have come to expect shopping ambience.

Project: Robinson's Department Store
Location: Costa Mesa, C
Client: The May Co., St. Louis
Design Firm: Hambrecht Terrell International, New York

Black accents provide a striking contrast to the muted tones of the walls and floor.

INTERIOR DESIGN TEAM:

Planner: George Bonet
Designers: James Terrell, Ed Calabrese
Decorator: John Hoch
Chairman: Edward Hambrecht
Lighting Design: Jann Weaver
President: James Terrell
Photographer: Jack Boyd

The ascending escalator well begins 30 feet wide on the first level and increases to 70 feet wide at the third floor, and is topped by two cascading skylights.

J. W. Robinson's café is sleekly sparse. The geometric skylight situated above the many-angled display case provides visual impact.

Another view of the cascading skylight, one of two in the store.

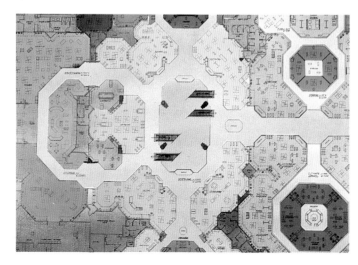

Floor plan

Black fixtures bring the viewer's eye directly to the merchandise displayed against the walls.

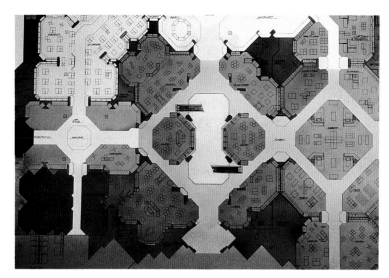

Floor plan

*Three-dimensional layered glass
provides an unusual design element in
this sophisticated cosmetics display.*

The store's sleek angular design is apparent in the China/Glassware Department. Note how the cascading skylight enhances the open feeling of this floor design.

Duty Free Shoppers' Ltd. Chinachem, Hong Kong

HONORABLE MENTION, New Full-Line Department Store

Designer: TSL Design Group

TSL Design Group's three principals—Tak Toda, Richard Lewis and Tsuyoshi Sugauchi (who heads the Group's Tokyo office)—established a Los Angeles-based interior design office that would turn out fresh and unique designs to meet the needs of the retail industry. It was a tall order, especially since retail design demands a steady stream of current, yet adaptable concepts to act as a backdrop for ever-changing merchandise.

Now in its fourth year, TSL had been satisfying the demands of the international retail design market. The firm has successfully met the diverse needs of both new and remodeling projects in stores, especially department stores and food markets. The team has provided novel solutions to design problems ranging from the remodeling and architectural documentation for a chain of seven high-end department stores in Southern California to the innovative interior design or the 72,000-square-foot flagship store for Duty Free Shoppers', Ltd., in the central Chinachem district of Hong Kong.

April 15, 1988, marked the opening of Duty Free Shopper's largest of its 150 stores. The Chinachem project set the standard in design for all DFS stores in 20 countries around the world. TSL considers this project most striking in its carefully developed traffic patterns. The two-story building is entered through the rear bus drop-off, where shoppers are guided up the escalator and through the five upper-floor departments. Flooring materials and carpeting mark the path into and around the retail sections, and then a second escalator descends to the remaining departments and building exits.

Imported materials are employed to address specific environments and to add to interior character. Circulation from department to department is defined by light and dark color and value. Rhythm from space to space is delineated by Italian marble and tile floors. Imported U.S. carpet indicates the various departments: Liquor/Tobacco/Perfume, Watches, Fine Jewelry, Leather Goods, Men's Accessories, Cosmetics, Apparel, and Oriental Gifts. Hard flooring in the aisles directs traffic within the soft and comfortable shopping "rooms," which include furniture and tables from Italy. American ready-to-wear fixtures and crown molding from Canada are also used. The rusted metals, patina finishes and lacquers contribute to the high-style design. TSL explains that all materials and fixtures were meticulously specified to define and maximize usable retail space.

Innovative visuals complement DFS' interior design and merchandise, as well as the city's local character. Daringly different from traditional retail display units, the Grand Mirage 3-D image projection unit exhibits products through a system of hidden mirror reflections in two locations.

In order to offer such ingenious visual presentations, TSL worked closely with in-house design directors Ron Bausman, DFS Corporate Visual Merchandising Director in San Francisco, and William Chan, Visual Merchandising and Construction Coordinator in Hong Kong.

Other eye-catching ornamental elements, such as large etched glass in the escalator/lobby areas and museum-quality wood sculptures and full-scale Chinese figure replicas, further enhance the pleasing and novel atmosphere of the store.

Project: Duty Free Shoppers
Location: Hong Kong
Client: D.F.S. International Ltd.
Design Firm: T.S.L. Design Group-Los Angeles/Tokyo

The fluorescent-lit handrail on the escalator guides shoppers through all departments.

INTERIOR DESIGN TEAM:

Planner:	T.S.L. Design Team
Designer:	T.S.L. Design Team
Decorator:	T.S.L. Design Team
Job Captain:	T.S.L. Design Team
Project Manager:	T.S.L. Design Team
Vice President in Charge:	T.S.L. Design Team
President/Chairman:	Tak Toda, I.S.P.
Consultants:	Lighting-Swarens Associates
Visual Presentation:	Ron Bausman-D.F.S., Corporate V.P. Director; William Chan-D.F.S., Hong Kong V.P. Mgr.
Photographer:	Paul Bielenberg

Fine materials, outstanding craftsmanship and oriental touches set a mood that distinguishes DFS from other stores.

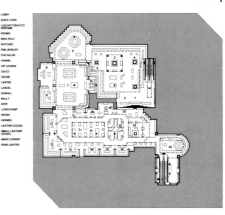

Floor plan

1 LOBBY
2 QUICK CARD
3 LIQUOR/TOBACCO/
   PERFUME
4 PROMO
5 NINA RICCI
6 WATCHES
7 FINE JEWELRY
8 FUR SALON
9 CHANEL
10 VIP LOUNGE
11 GUCCI
12 CELINE
13 CARTIER
14 LANCEL
15 DUNHILL
16 BALLY
17 DIOR
18 LONGCHAMP
19 SHOES
20 HERMES
21 LEATHER GOODS
22 SMALL LEATHER
   GOODS
23 MENS CORNER
24 PENS/LIGHTER

2F Duty Free Shoppers
Hong Kong/Chinachem

1 COSMETICS
2 PERFUMERY
3 COSTUME JEWELRY
4 SCARVES
5 LADIES FASHIONS
6 POLO
7 SUNGLASSES
8 DUNHILL
9 READY-TO-WEAR
10 ORIENTAL FASHIONS
11 EMBROIDERY
12 THEME SHOP
13 SOUVENIRS
14 ORIENTAL GIFTS
15 TOYS
16 SPORTS EQUIPMENT
17 DUTY PAID LIQUOR
18 PACKAGED FOODS
19 COOKIES/ICE CREAM

Floor plan

1F Duty Free Shoppers
Hong Kong/Chinachem

Fine Italian marble flooring enhances the Cosmetics Department

Different-colored flooring delineates "rooms," letting shoppers know when another department begins.

Printemps Denver, Colorado

Designer: Norwood Oliver Design Associates, Inc.

The challenger was European, the first foreign department store to enter the United States. How does a European department store in America develop an American merchandising point of view? How does that store fulfill the American dream of a European shopping experience? The solutions Printemps found included a number of ideas innovative to U.S. retail design.

Walls that do not touch the ceiling, undefined aisles, and limited use of carpeting are revolutionary design elements in a department store with 60,000 square feet of retail space. Open flowing spaces are free and are not dictated by typical retail foils; departments are not bordered by harsh walls and are not restricted by a particular colored carpet. Spaces without aisles or walls give way to a more human environment, where customers can move more freely.

To reinforce the open feeling, a grand staircase spirals through the center point of three levels, from bottom-floor bistro to upper-level retail. It intersects with the major cross-axes on both retail floors (leading to and from store entrances), thus controlling and defining the space. The stairwell is a central element with strong visibility. The softly carpeted stairs are bordered in black and point to a graceful cast-iron balustrade. Its Old World style and antique finish were custom designed for this project. Shops around the stairwell are drawn into its design, maintaining the spirit. About the staircase, barrel-vaulted ceilings curve softly.

The store was designed to serve as a backdrop for unique merchandising techniques. A meshing of light and form, fixed shelves and fixtures, floats merchandise to the customers. Private label hosiery is housed in library drawers with samples on display. Evening wear reaches any fashion length on adjustable telescoping fixtures. Clothing is presented with a "closet" approach, with garments hanging on rods and accessories lining the shelves. As a departure, Cosmetics uses showcases that are clean slabs of overlapping white tile. Built-in niches house testers and display products under glass; the slabs provide a natural accommodation for customer handbags. Lighting beneath the slabs creates an illusion of lightness and floating planes.

Crystal chandeliers provide a striking traditional formal counterpoint to the contemporary vernacular of the store.

On the main level, real stone floors lend a rich, natural aura, while overall carpeting on the second floor reinforces the feeling of space. Black crinkle-finish hardware adds impact to the merchandise while also framing it. Faux stone finish and white walls enhance openness.

The curving staircase is dramatic and beautiful.

Project: Printemps
Location: Denver, CO
Client: Hill Financial
Design Firm: Norwood Oliver Design Associates, Inc., New York

INTERIOR DESIGN TEAM:

Planner: Diane Sibert
Designer: Peggy Kiang
Decorator: Susan Starnes
Project Manager: Diane Koester
Vice President in Charge: Stephen Young
President/Chairman: Norwood Oliver
Consultant: John R. Wedum, in association with Au Printemps, Paris (Stair, facade design)
Visual Merchandising Director: Catherine Birkes, Printemps
Photographer: Larry Bollig

Floor plans

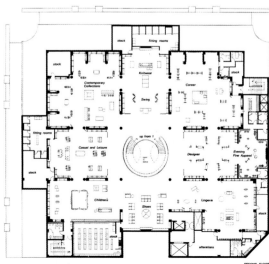

The black wrought-iron balustrade and crystal chandeliers provide a touch of Old World elegance.

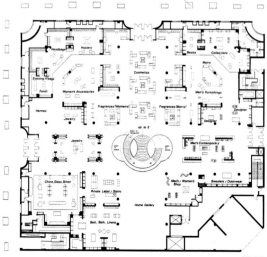

Crystal chandeliers provide a nice contrast to the ultra-modern cosmetic display cases.

The barrel-vaulted ceiling gives a
majestic look to the upper level of
Printemps.

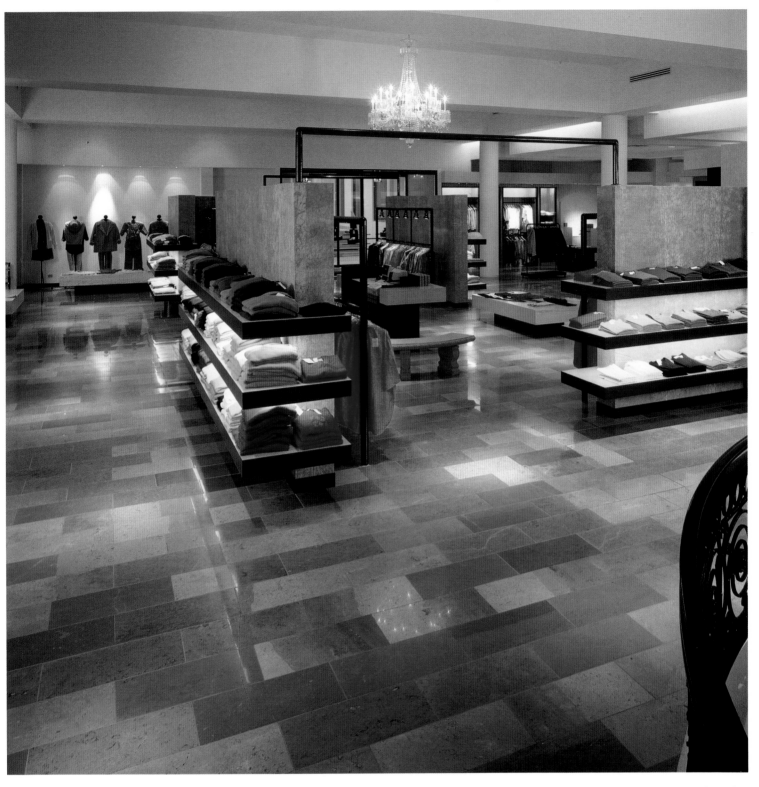

The undefined aisles and walls that do not reach the ceiling contribute an airy and fresh look.

Openness and clean, unencumbered displays show the European influence on Printemps.

The stone flooring reflects the light from fixtures, to provide a grand appearance.

chapter
12345
678

RENOVATED FULL LINE
DEPARTMENT STORE

Filene's
Chestnut Hill, Boston, Massachusetts

HONORABLE MENTION, Renovated Full-Line Department Store

Designer: Norwood Oliver Design Associates, Inc.

Design is the new strength of this remodeled retailer. The store's 150,000 square feet were totally gutted. With a dash of glitz and a lot of sophistication, the design put the emphasis on quality, since true quality suits the high-end attitude and the retailer's customer.

A classic-traditional style was created. Traditional took the upper hand, with interiors enhanced by chandeliers, moldings and wall coverings. The results are elegant and residential. But the objective was carried throughout the store, with "world concepts" that create a specialty-store appeal.

There is total identification in each world. In the men's space, herringbone-patterned wood aisles are unmistakably masculine. A strong beam treatment along the aisles leads to individual shops and visual presentations. Traditional moldings frame faux stone finishes.

The most impressive example of the world concept is the French Room, actually a series of shops. Rich ash and vanilla surroundings host European designer collections. A cozy cluster of residential furnishings helps set a definitive mood. Unifying the area, an aisle of creamy marble is shot with black diamonds and boarders. Design adapts to suit the shops, but the aisle remains constant. In one space, a barrel-vaulted ceiling dons silver leaf moldings and chandeliers. In another, a cove-lit ceiling contains moldings, crowns and classic columns. In all, gatherings of windows with mullions or glass paneling allow customers an exciting view of shop interiors.

In the fur salon, silver leaf moldings frame lilac moiré walls and provincial furnishings. Ribbed silk walls in rich honey and softly striped camelback sofas create a comfortable setting for designer shoes. Better Sportswear has electric appeal: Double ceiling beams lead to a Palladian arch topped with glass.

Cosmetics are centered among Women's and Men's Sportswear on the main floor. Colors and materials are light and clean; shape is flowing. Rows of brass striping follow a ceiling drop, while over the aisles, a silver leaf wallpaper rises to meet a contemporary beam ceiling. Showcases take new shape with rounded glass fronts that flow into glossy laminate. Top display pieces move back to afford a clear view of merchandise under the glass. Highly reflective elements on a white marble floor in a well-lit area create a unique effect. All these contribute to the sparkling quality of this wonderful space.

Project: Filene's
Location: Chestnut Hill, Boston
Client: Wm. Filene's & Sons, Co.
Design Firm: Norwood Oliver Design Associates, Inc., New York

INTERIOR DESIGN TEAM:

Planner: Frank Sluzas
Designer: John Blackwell
Decorator: Susan Starnes, Cynthia Davidson
Project Manager: Vera Cousineau
Vice President in Charge: Stephen Young
President/Chairman: Norwood Oliver
Lighting Consultant: Lumentech
Photographer: Stan Y. Kao

The diamond-studded, creamy marble floor of the "French Room" is sophisticated and elegant. Crystal chandeliers, barrel-vaulted ceilings, a cove-lit ceiling and classic columns make this department memorable.

Traditional home furnishings provide a comfortable note as well as provide a relaxed atmosphere in the grand surroundings of the "French Room."

Herringbone wood floors add a masculine touch to the Men's Department.

The designer Shoe Department takes on an "at home" atmosphere via the use of table lamps, comfortable sofas and subdued tones.

Beamed ceilings provide a nice contrast to the light-toned marble flooring.

The pendant fixture above this mannequin platform gives visual impact to the merchandise on display.

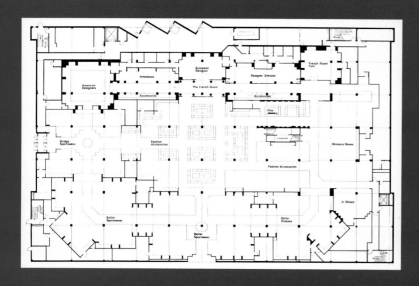

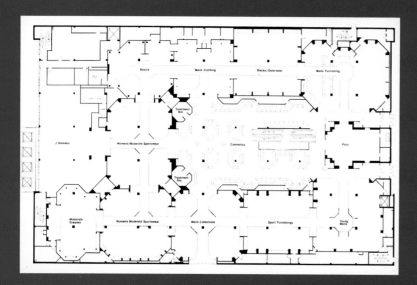

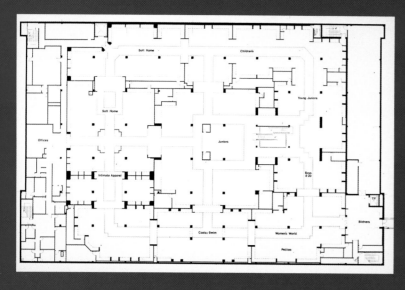

58 RENOVATED FULL LINE DEPARTMENT STORE

Fine materials and effective lighting provide the shopper with a pleasurable experience.

Dayton's

FIRST PRIZE, Renovated Full-Line Department Store

Designer: Tucci, Segrete & Rosen Consultants, Inc.

This retailer is in a major city landmark with over 600,000 square feet of space. The main floor covers almost a city block. Renovation took four years of dedication, compressing nine floors into six while increasing net selling space. But high-level service, logical merchandise assortment and simple flow-through circulation patterns inspired sales that surpassed projections. New aisles and floor plans increased the retailer's ability to move heavy traffic during peak hours.

Under the store is a classic market: 100,000 square feet containing a series of shops. Operable awning elements add charm while ensuring efficiency during lunch-hour business. The main aisle in ceramic tile hosts brick archways that align concourse entrances to Housewares, Flowers and more. Electronics is an envelope of black and gray, with green neon and digital signage. Home Textiles uses white stucco and bleached timbers, with terra-cotta aisles.

Grandeur in a classic style was key to the street-level restoration. Ceilings were maintained at full height, in a spacious environment landscaped with merchandise. Expansive crystal chandeliers crown a marble aisle, where customers peruse the cosmetics. The chandeliers bridge the spaces between cosmetics, shoes and accessories. Peach beveled mirrors add richness to island back fixtures.

The Juniors Department was designed for excitement. Architecture was exposed, restored and energized. Stainless-steel and copper railings thread through the terraced focal points.

The Men's Club, at the skyway level, occupies 90,000 square feet, with a configuration that segments everything from accessories and cosmetics to the finest tailored clothing, via travertine-bordered aisles. Classic dental moldings at the ceilings heighten the concept.

Above the skyway are two Women's Fashion levels. Following the elongated "L" configuration of the building, they are characterized by a grand aisle. On the third floor, it's paved with two colors of marble, with columns and ceiling panels, and hosts couture, famous designers and collections. In one shop, bleached Nordic oak with vertical slabs of glass updates the space, while a glass-block wall glows with neon backlighting that changes colors to suit the retailer's needs.

Sales confirm success. This design's esthetic appeal is truly contemporary, reaching major proportions.

Project: Dayton's Downtown
Location: Minneapolis, MN
Client: Dayton Hudson Corp.
Design Firm: Tucci, Segrete & Rosen, New York

INTERIOR DESGIN TEAM:

Designer:	Edward M. Calabrese
Decorator:	John Hock, Jr.
Project Director:	Evangelo Dascal
Executive Vice President in Charge:	Gerald Rosen
Principal in Charge:	Dominick Segrete
Sr. Vice President Dayton's Visual Merchandising, Dayton Hudson Store Planning Dept.:	Andrew Markopulos, Sr.
Photographer:	Jim Norris

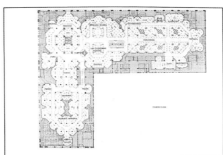

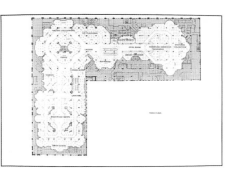

Modern outlined arches and aisle flooring resemble a playground, making the Children's Department playful and fun.

Elements used on the main floor are mainly traditional and elegant, to greet shoppers with a sophisticated ambience.

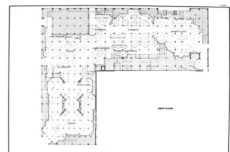

700 Under the Mall contains numerous shops that provide easy shopping for the lunchtime business crowd.

The design elements used in the Men's Department are masculine and appealing.

The third floor boasts two different colored marbles—one for the floor and one for the columns—a perfect backdrop for the Couture and Collection Departments.

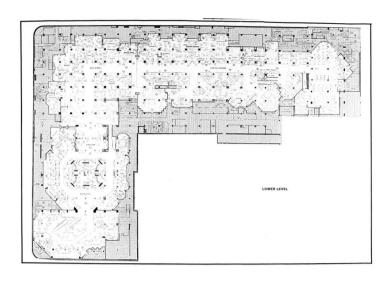

The etched glass, brass fittings and other fine materials help imbue the fourth floor with an upscale look.

Strawbridge & Clothier

FIRST PRIZE, Renovated Full-Line Department Store

Designer: The Pavlik Design Team

Rather than the luxury of working on a new building, this design firm started with a tired, old structure with two-level access from the parking area via a gangplank-style entrance.

The firm began the design from the inside out. This necessitated taking off the roof and removing one exterior wall, but resulted in a greater focus on customers and their shopping experience.

The objective was to build the most exciting, state-of-the-art department store in the country. This would be achieved by crediting better ideas in every merchandising classification and by projecting "Wow Merchandise Vistas."

The design excitement begins at the top, with the gabled roof at the center of the third floor, and continues down to the two-story grand entrance. There's a European-style Café that overlooks a replica of "Porcellino," the wild boar fountain from Florence, Italy. Suspended above the fountain is a large, 18th-century-style clock with scrollwork detail and brass trim. A vaulted skylight over the upper-level shipping area focuses light on two 9 foot Dutch murals, completing the theme of light and air in conjunction with classic style.

The original gangplank was removed and replaced by a 65-foot-high bridge from the parking lot to the store's middle level. This Neo-classic design is filled with greenery, trees, and benches; it incorporates the elements of classic style while using light and air to signify progress into the future.

The store has an easy-to-follow aisle system, with merchandise housed in many individual shops. It's a design based on small groupings rather than a sea of confusion. The project was created with the customer in mind. The ambience is unique on each of the three levels, offering the shopper more exciting experience.

Project: Strawbridge & Clothier
Location: King of Prussia, PA
Client: Strawbridge & Clothier
Design Firm: The Pavlik Design Team, Fort Lauderdale, FL

The grand entranceway.

INTERIOR DESIGN TEAM:

Planner:	Robert Leuchten
Project Designer:	Luis Valladares
Assistant Designer:	Fernando Castillo
Job Captain:	Hernando Acosta
Project Manager:	Alfredo Marriaga
Principal:	R. J. Pavlik
Lighting Consultant:	Theo Kondos
Contractor:	Barclay White Associates
Architect:	RTKL, Fort Lauderdale
Lighting Designer:	Constanza Kehren
Photographer:	Jim Norris

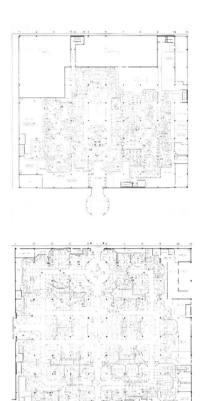

The gabled skylight and Dutch mural further promote a classical ambience.

Dental moldings and classical features are juxtaposed with modern mobiles in the Children's Department.

*Classical elements unify the
departments in the store.*

The large, 18th-century-style clock
adds a classical touch to the
European-style café.

Feminine and graceful columns flank the Lingerie Department.

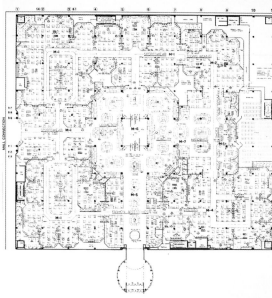

Light-colored marble and unobtrusive lighting support, rather than detract from, the merchandise in the Jewelry Department.

chapter

12345
678

**SPECIALTY DEPARTMENT
STORE OR SHOP IN A
DEPARTMENT STORE FOR
APPAREL AND / OR
ACCESSORIES**

Joseph Spiess Co. Randhurst Shopping Center, Mt. Prospect, Illinois

HONORABLE MENTION, Specialty Department Store or Shop for Apparel and/or Accessories

Designer: Schafer Associates, Inc.

Spiess is a small chain of department stores specializing in moderate , to bridge, to better fashion apparel. The customer base consists mainly of families in the middle to upper-income brackets. This Spiess store is a new construction and is an addition to a recently remodeled major shopping mall. The location is in a suburb of a major metropolitan area; the designer's challenge was to create a fresh look while retaining the familiarity and eloquent ambience of the established Spiess image.

The strongest element of the space is the core. The plan capitalizes on this with a simple ring-road circulation pattern that feeds traffic around and into the core via strong, bold entrances, complete with arched sign panels. The result is ease of circulation with emphasis toward the center from all areas. Aisle intersections are accented by lighted vitrine displays, customer comfort zones and special merchandise presentations. Beautiful marble flooring with borders accentuates the core and the comfort zones. A matte-finish ceramic tile provides a soft look for auxiliary traffic aisles.

The design of the core sets the tone for the retail environment. A 90-foot barrel-vaulted skylight opens up the center section, creating drama, elegance and sparkle. The perimeter walls of the core are partial height, letting light enter every area of the store and capturing the feeling of openness and daylight as well as a sensation that there is "always more beyond." Classic faux marble columns with decorative capitals flank the center aisles. A central clock tower provides a focal point as well as a meeting place. A grand piano sits below the clock, and customers can shop to live music emanating throughout the store.

Departments inside the core support the apparel businesses on the store's perimeter. Cosmetics, Accessories and Shoes have a similar feeling in design and use of materials. For example, a special "rice paper" glass is used on the shoe cubes as well as the private cosmetic consultation areas; this unification of design helps give customers a consistent message of quality and attention to detail. A small gourmet food section is yet another amenity within the core.

Perimeter departments are wide, shallow and easy to shop. Each has its own appropriate decor, appealing to a targeted customer. Ceiling heights taper down in these areas from the contrasting openness of the center core, making the apparel departments more intimate. State-of-the-art lighting techniques are used in all areas, incorporating the new octron fluorescent lamp. The overall result is a store with elegant ambience and customer-friendly details.

Project: Spiess, Randhurst
Location: Mount Prospect, IL
Client: Joseph Spiess & Co.
Design Firm: Schafer Associates, Inc., Oakbrook Terrace, IL

INTERIOR DESIGN TEAM:

Planner: Dale Payton
Designer: Schafer Associates Design Dept.
Job Captain: Greg Narlock
Project Manager: Dale Payton
Vice President in Charge: Ronald Lubben, S.I.S.P.
President/Chairman: Robert W. Schafer
Consultant: J. L. Carroll Associates
Suppliers: Ragner Benson, Park Ridge, IL; Store Kraft, Beatrice, NE; Commercial Store Fixtures, Grand Rapids, MI
Photographer: Jim Norris

The ceramic tile, white pole lamps and ice cream parlor-type tables and chairs lend a bistro feeling in the Misses Department.

The barrel-vaulted ceiling, large clock and ebony baby grand piano immediately alert the shopper to the quality of Spiess.

The Cube and Tiger Shop/ The Bon Marche

Bellevue Square, Bellevue, Washington

FIRST PRIZE, Specialty Department Store or Shop for Apparel and/or Accessories

Designer: The Bon Marche Store Planning Division, in collaboration with Robert Young Associates

The design objectives for this shop were based on the store's management's program for realignment. Included in the plans were relocation of several departments and elimination of others in approximately 50,000 square feet of the store's total 174,000 square feet. This put the Juniors and Young Men's Departments on the lower level, which was not a high-traffic location. The building code did not allow alteration, so for this concept to work, these areas had to become destination departments, with enough excitement to generate their own traffic. Attracting customers required a hi-tech approach.

The solutions began with design objectives. First, primary traffic patterns were established to draw people into the departments. Second, orientation of the rooms was modified to reinforce the direction of entry. Third, a secondary circulation pattern was created with implied aisles defined only by fixtures, thereby not diminishing the primary traffic patterns.

Next, the designers considered the targeted young customer. Each department's ceramic floor tile pattern was coordinated with the ceiling design. In Juniors, the ceiling cove was washed by multi-colored bands of traveling neon light that moves from the entrance into the department. All free-standing and perimeter fixtures were custom designed.

Decorations and finishes were also customized. The fixture hardware chosen has a charcoal hammer-tone finish and is used on all the metal grid systems. Selected walls and fitting rooms are painted with Zolatone. The majority of the walls in Juniors were painted with "veiling lacquer," a multi-coated custom finish with a gloss solid white background and a large-textured black-string spatter. The Young Men's area is accented with high-gloss lacquered fin walls with bullnosed edges.

Field porcelain tile in the Young Men's Department has a light gray matte finish; the aisle is polished light gray with textured matte and glossy granite border tile. The department core is a matte and glossy dark gray porcelain. The Junior's field tile is Armstone pepper white. The aisle is glossy white porcelain tile with a glossy black-and-white border. The dressing area has a marble tile insert. The only locations with carpeting are the shoe section and the fitting rooms.

Project:	The Bon Marche, Cube & Tiger Shops
Location:	Bellevue, WA
Client:	The Bon Marche
Design Firm:	Robert Young Associates, Inc.

INTERIOR DESIGN TEAM:

Project Designer:	Michael Wilkins
Project Managers:	Frank McMillin, Steve Van Landingham
Principal in Charge:	Robert Marks
President:	Robert Young
Neon Consultant:	Neotek
Color and Materials Design:	Hallie Galloway
Visual Merchandising Director:	Ron Spencer, The Bon Marche
Photographer:	Robert Pisano

Neon lights outline the perimeter of the ceiling, which mimics the aisle shape and the pattern in the floor, providing a unified, imaginative look in the Young Men's Department.

The Junior Department's ceiling cove is washed by multi-colored bands of traveling neon light, which moves from the entrance into the core of the department.

Current popular colors and ultramodern designs highlight areas throughout the store.

Harold

HONORABLE MENTION, Specialty Department Store or Shop for Apparel and/or Accessories

Designer: **Norwood Oliver Design Associates, Inc.**

Shopping in this specialty store is like being in an elegant, old mansion. Walk into the main gallery and you're in a luxurious foyer. Old World moldings and fine materials suggest the grand-manner; while the classic architecture is reinforced with antiques and wall sconces. Glass front doors of grand height, a magnificently sparkling chandelier and a warm interior create a gracious feeling as customers enter the shop. Harold has always been home to a high-end, service-oriented shopper. Here, customers and salespeople interact on a personal basis.

The first-floor hallway is a reception area where the merchandise is part of the design. Off the main entrance, where in a mansion would be salons and ballrooms, are the luxurious shops. The Tiffany Shop is a tiny room, but its 15-foot-high ceiling is impressive, with a chandelier illuminating the space. Merchandise is presented in displays reminiscent of antique collection showcases. The lighting contributes to the mood, with many coves and varying intensities.

The new design provides improved vertical circulation as well as delightful surprises. Walk into the main space, and the store begins to open to its full 40,000 square feet. The rooms (shops) are grand and more numerous than expected. A front staircase connects the first and second levels. In the old store, customers used back-area fire stairs instead of waiting for elevators. Now, a back staircase connects all four levels. Both staircases have decorative balustrades, oriental carpeting, chandeliers and tapestries on the walls.

On the second floor, a wide-open stairwell with a vaulted ceiling above provides views of the first level below. Pauses in the hallway, which would normally hold breakfronts, have been used for merchandise display.

The crowning jewel is on the fourth level. Like a Victorian parlor, Couture has furnishings that are museum quality. Customers are invited to sit and relax, while the merchandise is presented to them.

Hallways in this design are framed with creamy marble floors into which black columns have been set. They face a unique set of handcarved glass elevator doors, used here as decoration. Fitting rooms with generous 10 x 10-foot dimensions are also decorated with chandeliers and sconces.

		INTERIOR DESIGN TEAM:
Project:	Harold	
Location:	The Conservatory, Minneapolis	
Client:	Robert Dayton	
Design Firm:	Norwood Oliver Design Associates, Inc., New York	

Planner:	Diane Sibert
Designer:	John Blackwell
Decorator:	Susan Starnes
Project Manager:	Madan Vazirani
Vice President in Charge:	Stephen Young
President/Chairman:	Norwood Oliver
Photographer:	George Heinrich

The foyer provides a breathtaking first impression: a crystal chandelier, fine antique furniture, oriental carpeting and a comforting homelike feeling.

Tapestries grace the walls of the staircase, while fine architectural detailings imbue an elegant air.

Comfortable antique furniture bids the weary shopper to sit and rest.

Merchandise is displayed simply and elegantly.

Graceful touches and subtle colorings enhance the image of Harold.

Rooms open off the hallway, making customers feel as if they are in a friend's home.

The Shoe Salon is feminine and plush in rose velvets; antique porcelains grace the tops of display cases.

Fine moldings are painted a shade lighter than the walls to outline arches and doorway.

Wall sconces provide ambient lighting.

Parquet floors and oriental rugs add rich color and texture.

"Rooms" are defined off the aisles.

Anna Bassett's Claire Pearone
Somerset Mall, Troy, Michigan

FIRST PRIZE, Specialty Department Store or Shop for Apparel and/or Accessories

Designer: Jon Greenberg and Associates, Inc.

One of the most respected couture salons in the midwest successfully faced the challenge of renovation. It reduced the store's size by 35 percent, yet retained its grand ambience and merchandising flexibility.

Design changes included opening the store's whole front with floor-to-ceiling glass, with the exception of the stately architectural entrance. Colorfully veined marble was imported from Italy to create a strong visual statement that would greet customers as they enter through the glass doors. The same marble was used throughout the store as an accent on the perimeter, just above the merchandising line. Stark black-and-white marble tile was used at the entrance to help departmentalize the leather handbag and accessories area.

Light and airy in color, the store's interior is defined by geometrically chiseled drops above fashion vignettes and stonelike arches, giving focus to designer coordinates along the walls. Single-rod hanging in recessed fashion compartments extends the exclusive feeling that this environment creates.

Lighting is provided by incandescent spot lamps, both track mounted and recessed, and low-voltage, high-intensity fixtures. All accessory custom-designed display cases are lit from above, with no interior case lamps.

In the rear lower level, brass rails lead to evening wear. The area is punctuated by two vertical shadow display cases recessed into a black glass facade; higher-priced dresses are featured behind elegant glass doors and on custom glass floor fixtures. The store also features a refreshment bar on the lower level, near a bank of personally serviced fitting rooms.

Project: Anna Bassett's Claire Pearone
Location: Somerset Mall, Troy, MI
Client: Anna Bassett
Design Firm: Jon Greenberg & Associates, Inc.

INTERIOR DESIGN TEAM:

Planner:	Judy Norlin
Designers:	Kenneth Nisch, Elaine Albers, Judy Norlin
Decorator:	Elaine Albers
Project Manager:	Judy Norlin
President:	Kenneth Nisch
Construction Supervision:	JGA
Photographer:	Scott Sutton Photographic

The entrance to Anna Bassett's Claire Pearone is chic and upscale. An Italian veined marble facade and floor-to-ceiling glass doors greet the customer.

The color scheme is predominantly white and black, with mauve touches to focus attention on the merchandise.

In the Evening Wear Department, brass railings and five steps down define the area. Better dresses are locked behind glass doors that provide both security and visibility.

**SPECIALTY DEPARTMENT
STORE OR SHOP IN
A DEPARTMENT STORE
FOR HARD GOODS,
HOME FURNISHINGS,
CHINA, ETC.**

Bank One
Financial Marketplace Dublin, Ohio

FIRST PLACE, Specialty Department Store or Shop for Hard Goods, Home Furnishings, China, etc.

Designer: Retail Planning Associates, Inc.

This 5,500-square-foot full-service financial "supermarket" was to be a prototype for a new approach to the merchandising of financial services. The store was aimed at an affluent, contemporary market and would be open 72 hours a week, including Sundays. Retail planning and design techniques helped achieve this objective.

Financial institutions must compete in an increasingly retail atmosphere, and the supermarket setting, where consumers can get all their needs taken care of in one place, is the wave of the future. This design demonstrates strategic positioning and appropriate design can attract customers.

The merchandising concept builds product awareness through eight delineated financial services "boutiques." The boutiques allow customers to sense the tangibility of the services—in effect, allowing customers to "touch and feel" the bank's offerings. The teller transaction area was placed at the rear to draw customers through the space, exposing them to perimeter services as well as the "merchandise" information center.

The design utilizes the bank's corporate blue, including the neon boutique identifiers. Other materials include marble, porcelain pavers and carpet for flooring, laminates and natural woods. Standard-modular office panels are incorporated into the design, including backlit transparencies that help identify each service boutique. Dramatic lighting and natural light from a center skylight complete the effect.

Project: Bank One
Location: Columbus, OH
Client: Bank One
Design Firm: Retail Planning Associates, Inc., Columbus, OH

INTERIOR DESIGN TEAM:

Planner: Ken Chance
Designer: Ken Chance, Gary Kaiser
Job Captain: David Clary
Project Manager: Arnie Thies
Vice President in Charge: Bill Wood (Officer in Charge)
President/Chairman: Bruce Krysiak
Lighting Consultant: Larson Engineering
Graphic Designer: Matt Rumora, Tim Bachman
Architect: Bohm-NBBJ, Columbus, OH

The boutiques are laid out along the perimeter, with a central space that allows freedom of movement and a place to rest. The corporate blue dominates the space.

Backlit transparency panels mark the Realtor and Home Financing boutique. Carpeting and modular office panels also delineate each space.

A view of two additional boutiques. Neon signage provides immediate identification.

The central skylight is visible in this photograph. Note the open, airy effect.

The main entrance to the marketplace.

One of the main counters shows the predominant use of the corporate logo and the corporate color.

Counters provide a convenient and neat way to present literature.

The entrance to Bank One Financial
Marketplace.

*Backlit transparencies placed along the
perimeter of the ceiling is an effective
way to add life and decoration without
cluttering scarce wall space.*

Grand Rental Station Virginia Beach, Virginia

HONORABLE MENTION, Specialty Department Store or Shop for Hard Goods, Home Furnishings, China, etc.

Designer: Retail Planning Associates, Inc.

Grand Rental Station was a new concept in the rental industry. It aimed to provide an adaptable setting for its dealers nationwide, who have extremely variable rental merchandise mixes, but it also wanted a setting conductive to increased retail sales. The design had to be in concert with the company's red, white, gray, and blue color scheme, as well as compatible with its hardware store and home-center dealer programs. The name had been chosen and put into use, but the concept had no image.

The design takes advantage of the pre-existing name, with a look that resembles an 1800s small-town train station. The prairie design features roof overhangs and supporting arches, from which signage hangs. In this manner, the name was tied to the exterior.

Because all items could not be practically displayed in the retail-rental front room, there had to be a back room almost equal to the 2900-square-foot front room. The back room also had to accommodate areas for washing, cleaning and repairing equipment. In the front room, the design grouped retail tools and party rental goods in one area, using black-striped racetrack circulation to help create two different "worlds." On the

right side are the tools, contractor items, and lawn and garden equipment, while the left side features home, party, and banquet goods. The center island is a "swing focal" area to make major seasonal statements. Thus, the design gave more exposure to the store's entire product line.

All stock is one-item presentation; there is no bulk stock. Therefore, to give merchandise a "home" on the floor, 3 x 3-inch H-pattern freestanding fixture modules were custom-designed. The modules not only created a flexible way to work around the different-size products but also, when the modules were placed end to end, could make a gondola-type presentation. The fixtures are set upon dot-patterned gray Pirelli rubber flooring, which helps to highlight the presentation and is extremely durable and easily cleaned (an important consideration when dealing with greasy tools).

On the wall and freestanding fixtures, merchandise is presented on 1-inch Uniweb continuous metal wall paneling, which offers continuous flexibility and strength for an incredible range of products, from a 200-pound chain to lift automobiles to lawnmowers and compressors—all of which no longer are limited to floor

presentation.

With effective use of space and a distinctive graphic system, this design reinforces the combined rental-retail strategies while making it easier for customers to understand how the store functions.

Project: Grand Rental Station
Location: Virginia Beach, VA
Client: American Hardware
Design Firm: Retail Planning Associates, Inc., Columbus, OH

INTERIOR DESIGN TEAM:

Planner:	Butch Belszek
Designer:	Butch Belszek
Job Captain:	Mike Murphy
Project Manager:	Mike Murphy
Sr. Vice President in Charge:	Mike Murphy
President/Chairman	Bruce Krysiak
Merchandiser:	Barbara Engel
Graphic Designer:	Ed Grunewald
V.P., Lighting:	Vince Faiella
Photographer:	Robert Krusey

The rental station resembles an old fashioned train station.

Floor plan

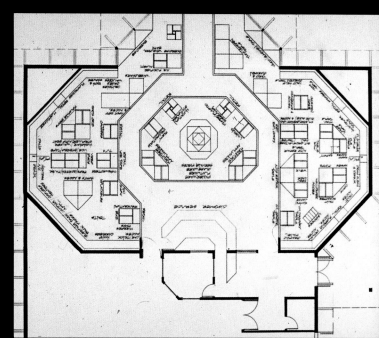

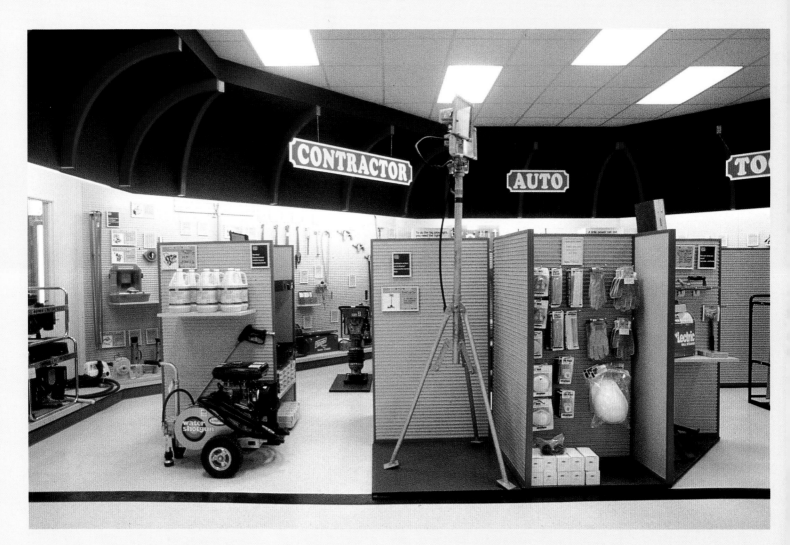

Freestanding H-shape modules allow merchandise to be presented in a gondola manner and permit the retailer to display varying sized merchandise simultaneously.

On one side of the store are retail tools, contractor items, and garden accessories; the other side features home, party, and banquet rental items.

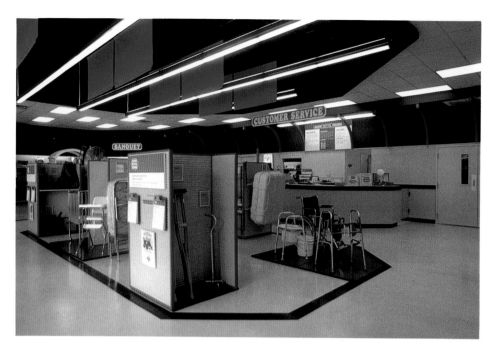

The geometric shapes created by the modules draw the viewer's attention to the merchandise being displayed.

The customer service desk is highly visible and centrally located.

The module presentation provides an uncluttered, clean look.

chapter

1 2 3 4 5
6 7 8

SUPERMARKETS, SPECIALTY FOOD RETAILING, FOOD COURTS, CONVENIENCE STORES

T. W. Best
Northwestern Atrium Center, Chicago, Illinois

FIRST PRIZE, Supermarkets, Specialty Food Retailing, Food Courts, Convenience Stores

Designer: Eva Maddox Associates, Inc.

This 1100-square-foot newsstand is located in a major train station. The client wanted to create a unique environment that would take the traditional newsstand into a new realm of retailing. The design would become the prototype for a series of smaller stores of different configurations, and would also be modified for a luxury hotel situation.

The newsstand accommodates a high volume of shoppers, so angled placement of the main candy display helped draw customers into the store and separate traffic and product zones. The design team turned an overlooked area into an opportunity for exciting colors, forms, finishes and spatial volumes.

The architectural framework allowed presentation of different product types throughout the store. Ceiling banners and beam elements visually articulate pathways and draw people into the space. Special "focus displays" allow a high density of a featured product to be displayed.

The design module was adaptable to smaller locations. This particular location is only 340 square feet and features a movable kiosk, which slides into the public area to display candy and newspapers. And when the prototype was modified for the hotel situation, designers used a soft color scheme and wood finishes.

After the initial roll-out and renovation of existing stores, sales reports showed significant volume increases. This reinforces the value of design in a mass-market situation.

Project: T.W. BEST/Eastern Lobby Shops
Location: Northwest Atrium Center, Chicago
Client: T.W. Best/Levy Organization
Design Firm: Eva Maddox Associates, Inc., Chicago

INTERIOR DESIGN TEAM:

Designer: Mary Beth Rampolla
Project Manager: J.D. McKibben
Vice President in Charge: Patrick H. Grzybek
President: Eva L. Maddox
Supplier: Inter Ocean Cabinet Company
Photographer: Jon Miller, Hedrich Blessing

Vibrant colors and space-age geometric forms make these modules distinctive.

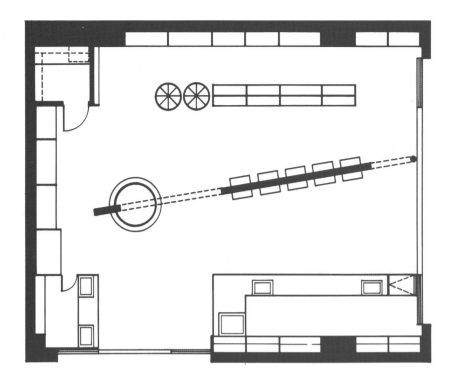

These modified versions of the brightly colored modules are more subdued, in light wood tones and soothing pastels.

Ceiling banners and beam elements clearly mark entrances and aisles.

The special-focus displays allow large quantities of an item to be displayed without appearing crammed or cluttered.

Merchandise is easily accessible, and the bright colors draw shoppers into the store.

Marui Imai
Sapporo Food Floors, Sapporo, Japan

FIRST PRIZE, Supermarkets, Specialty Food Retailing, Food Courts, Convenience Stores

Designer: Chaix & Johnson International, Inc.

Marui Imai's Sapporo Food Floors were the last phase in a series of renovations of their flagship store. The store consisted of 12 floors (including two basement floors: Basement 2 is a Confectionery/Grocery; Basement 1 is Fresh Foods/Gourmet) in the Annex Building and 11 floors (including a basement floor that has four restaurants) in the Main Building.

The design objective for this renovation was to create a "fashionable" urban department store—a trend setter, yet very refined. Important to the planning was to develop easy customer circulation and a strong first impression in each department.

Lighting was also an important element. The designers created the food floors to capture the feeling of a jewelry department. Fluorescent lighting on the ceilings and recessed lighting for fixtures provide a softer atmosphere, while strong accent lights illuminate the freshness of the food with a theatrical effect.

The approach was to emphasize simplicity in a modern environment. By utilizing soft as well as strong pastel colors, combined with textured and glazed tile, the designers created innovating architectural elements. Complemented by subdued color and texture, simplicity within a modern environment was achieved.

Project: Marui Imai-Sapporo Food Floors
Location: Sapporo, Japan
Client: Marui Imai Company, Inc.
Design Firm: Chaix & Johnson, Los Angeles

INTERIOR DESIGN TEAM:

Planner: Jin Higuchi
Designer: Masako Inoue
Decorator: JoAnn Nakamura
Job Captain: Renae Ilawkos
Project Manager: Jin Higuchi
Principal in Charge: Wayne Takeuchi
Chairman: Jin Higuchi

The simplistic design and basic color scheme provide a modern environment.

The shape of the display cases is mimicked in the ceiling directly above, providing dramatic, visual impact.

エレベーター →

*Pastel pink distinguishes the Bakery/
Confection Shop from the rest of the
"departments."*

Floor plan

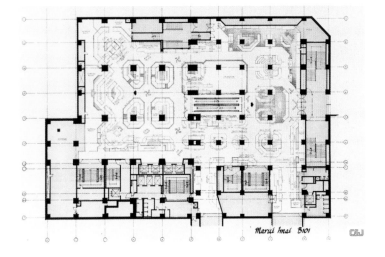

Geometric display cases, softly lit by
fluorescent ceiling fixtures and
recessed fixture lights, provide a
hushed, sophisticated feel.

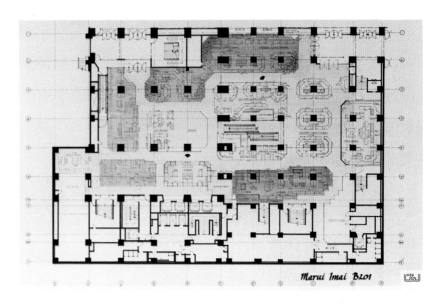

Floor plan

MASS MERCHANDISERS, DISCOUNT STORES, DRUG STORES

The Good Guys! Clearance Center

Quimby, San Jose, California

FIRST PRIZE, Mass Merchandisers, Discount Stores, Drug Stores

Designer: Retail Planning Associates, Inc.

The design objective was to develop a low-cost, flexible environment for today's value-driven consumer that would "dignify" the high-volume selling of returned, reconditioned, discontinued, closeout, overstocked, demo and "scratch and dent" goods of the 14-store mass merchandiser. This would be a fun, exciting atmosphere to counter the stereotypical image of a clearance center. The retailer wanted to tell consumers: "You don't have to shop in a 'down and dirty' atmosphere to get a good price!"

To provide flexibility, the designer made all fixtures adjustable and movable; most are on casters. Low-cost materials are used throughout the 12,000-square-foot selling area, most notably the warehouse rack and shelving system, which for this manufacturer was the first use in a selling environment. Circulation and merchandising are accented by a dropped ceiling grid and exposed HVAC overdrive aisles. Circulation areas are also differentiated from departments by varying colors and patterns of inexpensive vinyl flooring.

One innovative solution is the self-reeling electrical and antenna cords that hang from the ceiling to allow equipment to be tested in position, avoiding the high cost of electrifying every fixture or running conduit through the floor. For audio and VCR merchandise, which needs to be connected to a speaker and monitor, the designer created a test center, using it as a focal point to allow shoppers to hear and see electronics in working order while saving the cost of installing switching devices, as typical in most stores.

Colors are dominated by the sea-foam green fixtures and overhead grid, accented by red and yellow signage. Lighting helps achieve the dignified selling atmosphere because it is reminiscent more of a department store than a discounter.

While the design is low cost, it is tasteful and suitable for the merchandising and marketing objectives as well as project function.

Project: Good Guys
Location: San Jose, CA
Client: Good Guys
Design Firm: Retail Planning Associates, Inc., Columbus, OH

INTERIOR DESIGN TEAM:

Planner:	Mike Murphy
Designer:	Karen Cicenas
Job Captain:	Mike Murphy
Project Manager:	Mike Murphy
Sr. Vice President in Charge:	Mike Murphy
President/Chairman:	Bruce Krysiak
Lighting Consultant:	Vince Faiella, V.P., Lighting
Graphic Designer:	Karen Cicenas
Photographer:	Robert Krusey

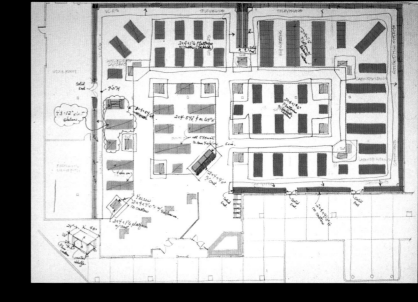

The entrance sets the tone for this clearance center.

The geometric pattern is established at the main entrance.

Steel shelving provides adequate display and storage space.

Stereo equipment is displayed in a test center, which provides a focal point for shoppers to hear equipment while the store saves the cost of installing switching devices.

The predominant colors are sea-foam green, red, and yellow.

The geometric floor pattern mirrors the geometric ceiling grid.

All fixtures are on casters to provide easy mobility.

Mervyn's Dublin, California

FIRST PRIZE, Mass Merchandisers, Discount Stores, Drug Stores

Designer: Retail Planning Associates, Inc.

The design goals for this 85,000-square-foot (gross)/62,000 (net) store were to provide a revolutionary, exciting design and a flexible concept that worked with Mervyn's promotional department store operating mode (that is, a new sale event every week) and to improve operating efficiencies and self-service in a store that stresses merchandise dominance in an easy-to-shop format.

To show the customer what Mervyn's stands for, the designer created separate "worlds," with departments clearly separated by color, texture and design. Yet the space remained open, so that a specialty-store (vs. department store) atmosphere results. The six distinct worlds include Home, Children's, Men's, Women's, Young World, and Accessories. The Young World, in the center of the store, combines Juniors and Young Men's in an upbeat environment akin to a specialty store within the store.

The interior design incorporates mannequins, architectural modular focal points and a bright white palette splattered by "shots" of bright colors. As a result, merchandise pops off the walls and tells the story. The bright color maximizes lighting effectiveness and efficiency, too. To add design flair and reinforce the traffic pattern, the ceiling drops over the aisles are made of a cost-effective bull nose-shaped modular formed fiberglass. The custom carpet incorporates the colors in a confetti pattern.

The store features flexible design elements. For example, walls, which are laminate covered and form a durable skin system, can be changed very quickly by moving divider panels, cubes and hardware. They are merchandised to 10 feet vs. 7½ feet previously, which adds color and has impact. All fixtures are on wheels, except cubes and shelving. New perforated metal fixtures in "strike points" are used to feature special promotional and fashion stories. These natural-colored "strike points" are 2 x 12-foot flexible zones that can be used for goods from any area of the store and create an ambience with special fixtures, lighting and graphics.

Ease-of-shopping considerations in the design include centralized cash wraps and a "C" channel for graphics that surrounds the perimeter and provides fast facts on products, prices and sizes. Unique neon departmental graphics form backlit silhouettes, signage and a neon tube to show cosmetics, shoes, housewares and so forth.

While upscaling the appearance and providing a dramatically different stage for displaying merchandise, the designer was careful not to make the look so upscale that customers would think the merchandise more expensive. Instead, the look is of value—appropriate to Mervyn's market position between a traditional department store and a traditional discounter.

Project: Mervyn's
Location: Dublin, CA
Client: Dayton Hudson Corp.
Design Firm: Retail Planning Associates, Inc., Columbus, OH

INTERIOR DESIGN TEAM:

Planner:	Nick Baughman, Eric Axene
Designers:	Dan Lynn, Brian Shafley
Project Manager:	Paul Pizzini
Vice President in Charge:	Bill Sands
President/Chairman:	Bruce Krysiak
Lighting Consultants:	Larson Engineering
Graphic Designer:	Tim Bachman
Technician:	Craig Nowakowski
Photographer:	Robert Krusey

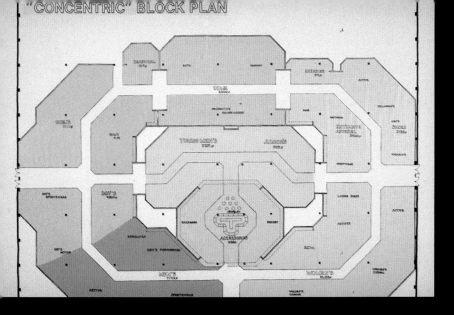

"CONCENTRIC" BLOCK PLAN

The entrance to Mervyn's

Neon signage welcomes shoppers to the Juniors world.

Perforated metal fixtures in "strike points" are used to feature special promotional and fashion stories.

Walls can be changed quickly by moving divider panels, cubes and hardware.

Mannequins are used in architectural,
modular focal points.

The predominant color is white, with dots of bright colors.

Anttila Department Store   Finland

FIRST PRIZE, Mass Merchandisers, Discount Stores, Drug Stores

Designer: Retail Planning Associates, Inc.

The design objectives for this 60,000-square-foot Finnish store were to re-allocate space based on selling productivity ratios, to develop an image of fashion leadership and to combine the best of European integrated fixture-intensive, one-source design with the best of U.S. design and merchandise-presentation techniques.

Changes for the three-floor facility involved enhancing the traditional basement food area, re-allocating storewide spaces and departmental groupings, creating a second-floor Home World, re-allocating cash wraps and installing a new escalator to the second floor. This was a total gutting of the 5 & 10-style table display retail approach.

Fixture choices were limited to a single supplier's package. But by taking advantage of stock space below the previous display tables, designers found a way to display more merchandise. The flexible fixturing designed and developed for the store accommodated the broad range of merchandise and became its market image, and largely its total new design and decor.

Core fixturing consisted of a three-foot square metal grid that runs overhead and along the perimeter of every department. The grid not only reinforces the circulation pattern but

also anchors the metal wall paneling. Boxes formed by the grid hold snap-in light fixtures, lower the effective 16-foot ceiling height and keep the shopper's eye down on the merchandise, soften the effect of exposed fluorescent strip lighting and accommodate illuminated panels that feature life-style photo murals. Photo murals also function in place of department signage.

The other main part of the fixturing system consists of square-punched metal perforated panels, similar to pegboard or slatwall. These panels can be used in a variety of ways: tall, wide panels can be hooked into the overhead grid to form department walls; when inserted into a base, the panels can be used as freestanding fixtures; and narrower pieces of the panels can be hooked to the gridwork, functioning as promotional displays. The fixtures that hang from these panels are interchangeable. The retailer has total display flexibility, and nearly the entire store (90 percent) could be fixtured at a cost of $10-$15 per square foot vs. $25-$75 per square foot for a typical U.S. department store.

Merchandise was to account for most of the color in the store and the plan was to use color subtly. Teal helps tie the store together and is used in

the new logo, in the color striping on the store's exterior, at cash wraps, in the food area and in fixturing for giftware, housewares, wicker and furniture. Color is also added by using pastel promotional fixtures, colorized to correspond to the department in which the fixtures are located. The remainder of the fixture paneling systems used in the store are off-white. For ease of maintenance and practicality in this land of snow, all flooring is hard surfaced. Terrazzo and tile were used on the food floor, vinyl wood flooring was used for aisles on the top two floors and vinyl tile was used in departments in a 1-meter-square pattern that reverses itself between soft and hard lines.

This is an extremely cost-effective, flexible solution to the renovation of a traditional European department store. While relying on traditional European idea of fixtures, the store does not come off as fixture-intensive, since the designer took great care to balance design philosophy with imaginative solution.

Project: Anttilla
Location: Tampere, Finland
Client: Anttilla
Design Firm: Retail Planning Associates, Inc., Columbus, OH

INTERIOR DESIGN TEAM:

Planner:	Mike Murphy
Designer:	Brian Shafley
Job Captain:	Mike Murphy
Project Manager:	Mike Murphy
Sr. Vice President in Charge:	Mike Murphy
President/Chairman:	Bruce Krysiak
Lighting Consultant:	Larson Engineering
Merchandiser:	Jane Zulandt
Technician:	Jim Penn
Photographer:	Mike Murphy

The merchandise provides the main color in the store.

Vinyl wood flooring is a practical material for a country where snow predominates most of the year.

The overhead grid has impact and separates departments.

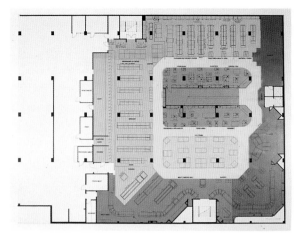

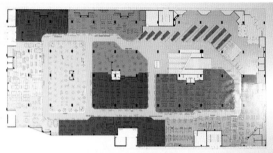

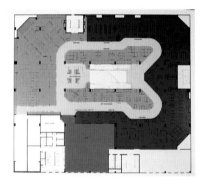

Floor plans

Teal is the sole accent color and is the corporate color.

Brands of Indiana Michigan City, Indiana

HONORABLE MENTION, Mass Merchandisers, Discount Stores, Drug Stores

Designer: Chicago Design Group, Ltd.

The owners of this 10,000-square-foot factory outlet store, specializing in moderate to high-end fashion clothing offered at discount prices, wanted a unique and different concept with a theme that could be used as a prototype for their retail outlet chain.

The design objective was to recreate the inside of an actual clothing factory, where merchandise is assembled before it is shipped to the retailer. To achieve the proper atmosphere, the factories of several clothing manufacturers were visited and photographs were taken. The photographs were used as part of the decor, along with memorabilia and artifacts donated and purchased from the manufacturers whose merchandise is displayed in the store.

Featured among the artifacts used for display purposes are a series of old and new carts and racks, conveyor belts, drop bins, mannequins, patterns, bolts of thread, sewing machines, bobbins, presses, ticking machines and cutting tables. The cash wrap is actually a series of cutting tables and dump bins, with a showcase on top to display the smaller merchandise. Other memorabilia include wooden chairs and tables.

Graphics and signage identifying clothing manufacturers such as Greif Mfg. Co. (representing Lavin, Polo, Chapps, Ralph Lauren and Perry Ellis), M. Liman Mfg., Leroy Seaters, Lakeland Mfg. Co., and Sanyo Mfg. Co. hang above the area displaying the particular merchandise from these manufacturers.

Industrial lighting fixtures were used, as well as industrial shelving on casters. All the racks have metal industrial panels capable of attaching bins, shelving and grid fixtures for storage of clothing. The industrial shelving consisted of plain lacquered wood and particle board, typical of factory shelving. A combination of industrial incandescent lamps tied into track lighting as well as fluorescent lights hang from an exposed-truss ceiling with exposed wood beams. Cables and rope also hang from this exposed factory-type ceiling.

The floor is tongue-and-groove, low-grade polished wood, and the walls are drywall and brick partitions. The fitting room doors were painted red and have raised panels. Safety tape was used on the floor to delineate aisles. The result is a most unusual factory outlet store resembling an actual clothing manufacturing factory.

Project: Brands
Location: Michigan City, IN
Client: Brands of Indiana
Design Firm: Chicago Design Group, Ltd., Northbrook, IL

INTERIOR DESIGN TEAM:

Planner: Kelly Smith
Design Director: Stephen Libbin
Decorator: Kelly Smith
Project Coordinator: Stephen Libbin
Display: Darby Epstein
Graphics & Signage: Sandy Krasovec
Contractor: Tonn & Blank
Suppliers: Parsteel (display fixtures); Total Lighting Concepts (Lighting)
Photographer: Walt Bukva Photographers

The design objective for this store was to recreate an actual clothing factory.

Brands signage.

Safety tape marks the aisles.

Antique dumps and bins provide a convenient storage space.

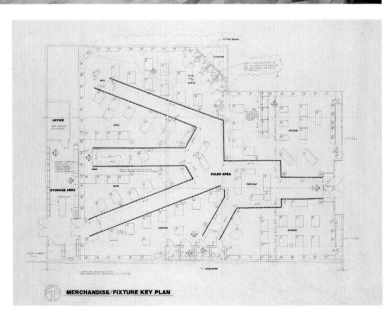

Floor plan

Clothing manufacturers' artifacts are used to further promote the "factory" image.

Carts hold merchandise.

Industrial lighting fixtures are used.

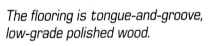

*The flooring is tongue-and-groove,
low-grade polished wood.*

Cables and rope hang from the exposed factory-type ceiling.

The industrial shelving consists of plain
lacquered wood and particle board.

Graphics and signage identify the various manufacturers of the merchandise on display.

Fitting room doors are painted bright red.

chapter

12345 678

APPAREL AND/OR ACCESSORIES STORES UNDER 5000 SQUARE FEET

Xani

 Bridgewater Commons, Bridgewater, New Jersey

HONORABLE MENTION, Apparel and/or Accessories Stores Under 5,000 Square Feet

Designer: **The International Design Group (USA), Inc.**

Xani is the result of a process of design and construction that has progressed over three years and in three stores. The concept encapsulates the needs of the client to sell costume jewelry in an identifiable environment. Xani attracts high-ticket clientele while not intimidating the $5 customer.

The store had an open plan, allowing the purchaser to wander comfortably among a combination of showcase and museum case displays. Wall cases, which are notched into the perimeter walls, provide a dramatic backdrop. A major design feature of Xani is the column display spinners. The sloping bulkhead and pedestals provide an interesting and functional alternative to conventional counter-type earring displays. Museum cases, which are on top of rolling carts, are feature elements that give glitz and sparkle to the overall look of the store. Each glass cube provides a stage to allow the client to present merchandise of varying themes and trends. The base of each cube has a locking sliding drawer, which enables the client to remove one side of the cube and its bed pad for easy access. The result is a flexible unit that is freestanding mechanically as well as conceptually.

Xani is one of the first retail stores to utilize Avonite, a horizontal surfacing material, in a nonconventional way. The storefront is predominantly of this very durable material. The overall effect is an entry of grand scale and presence. The dramatic carpet against the subtle hues of mauve adds a distinguishable contrast to the character and identity of Xani.

Project: Xani
Location: Bridgewater, Commons, NJ
Client: Wayne & Laurie LeMontang
Design Firm: The International Design Group (USA) Inc., New York

INTERIOR DESIGN TEAM:

Design Director: Ruth Mellergaard
Job Captain: Colette Trettin
Project Manager: Ruth Mellergaard
Consultant: Charles Z. Fertig, P.E.
Contractor: R. C. Pazur Construction

The entrance has an effect on a grand scale.

Xani's storefront is constructed predominantly of Avonite, a horizonta surfacing material.

Floor plan

Museum cases on rolling carts are main feature elements.

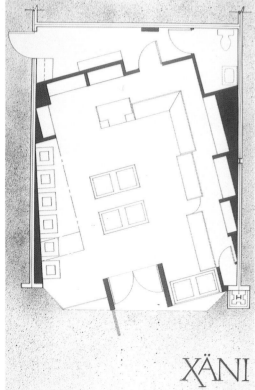

Column display spinners are a main design feature of Xani.

The Xani design allows customers to wander about freely.

Kids 'N Action Pleasanton, California

HONORABLE MENTION, Apparel and/or Accessories Stores Under 5,000 Square Feet

Designer: Gensler and Associates/Architects

Kids 'N Action is a prototypical children's store in Stoneridge Mall, Pleasanton, California. The merchandising approach and market niche identified by the owner are children's "activity" toys and action-related items. The owners plan to develop 50 additional Kids 'N Action stores nationally. They perceive a yet-untapped market among sports-minded parents, who will purchase sports-related items, toys and clothing for their children.

The team approached the prototype design by creating a whimsical neighborhood from a child's point of view. An open and dramatic storefront utilizes a faux stone gateway flanked by a white picket fence. A flying metal-ribbon sign identifies the entrance to the neighborhood. Eight-foot-high town facades constructed at slightly different angles to each other create interesting merchandise presentations and provide additional storage space. The facades represent a variety of community buildings—a ballet school for dancewear, a gas station for riding toys and a pet shop for animal squeeze toys. Each was built to feature the variety of merchandise categories.

To avoid the hard look of fluorescent lighting, the designers kept the walls well below the ceiling plane and incorporated fluorescent tubes at the top edge for soft ambient lighting. Supplementary track lighting highlights specific merchandise displays.

Finally, all wall surfaces were painted by an artist to create soft, abstracted surfaces depicting the appropriate building textures and neighborhood greenery. The color palette is restricted to white and pastel tones to present a noncompetitive backdrop for the primary colors of the youthful merchandise.

Project: Kids 'N Action
Location: Pleasanton, California
Client: Betsy Gordon, Andrew Hyman
Design Firm: Gensler and Associates/Architects, San Francisco

INTERIOR DESIGN TEAM:

Design Director: Ronette King
Project Director: Charles Kridler
Vice Presidents in Charge: Charles Kridler, Ronette King
Design Team: Warner Wong, Kuei-Ting Yang, John Bricker, Tom Horton
General Contractor: Fisher Development, Inc.
Artist: Laurie Lambertson
Storefront: Dixson Sign Company
Photographer: Sharon Risedorph

The entrance to Kids 'N Action is marked by two stonelike pillars and a small picket fence.

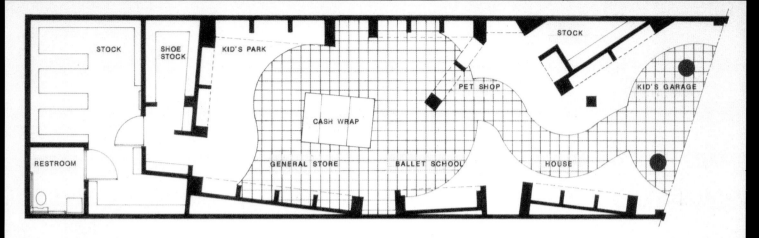

KIDS 'N ACTION

STONERIDGE MALL, PLEASANTON, CA.

1300 SQUARE FEET

Floor plan

Kids 'N Action utilizes a whimsical neighborhood from a child's point of view as the main design element. Here, animal toys are displayed in the Pet Shop.

Each type of merchandise is displayed in a different neighborhood store.

A multicolored tile path leads shoppers through the neighborhood.

chapter

12345
678

HARD GOODS AND/OR
HOUSEWARES STORES
UNDER 5000 SQUARE FEET

Fuller Brush
Town East Mall, Mesquite, Texas

FIRST PRIZE, Hard Goods and/or Housewares Stores Under 5,000 Square Feet

Designer: Retail Planning Associates, Inc.

A household name since 1906, Fuller Brush, which had been test marketing its range of new and innovative products via a newly created catalog, sought to complement this marketing effort by opening a chain of stores. The stores would be located primarily in malls and secondarily in strip centers. The company's goal was to create a contemporary store image that would effectively communicate cleanliness, efficiency and quality. The prototype store was also to be memorable and serve as the signature look for the chain—one consumers would instantly recognize.

Although the client did not place design constraints on the concept per se, a major consideration was the ability to display a variety of dissimilar products ranging from the famous hairbrushes to mops and brooms, cooking accessories, linens and so on in an organized environment. While doing so, the space had to remain flexible enough to accommodate new and innovative merchandise. Finally, while the client wanted a contemporary environment, the Fuller Brush "heritage" was also to be incorporated.

The plan was to expose as much merchandise as possible to customers viewing the store from a mall. To do so, the designers used 45°-angled interior walls to define several "worlds" (closet organizers, kitchenwares, personal-care items and cleaning products) within the smallish 2500-square-foot space. New and fashion products and colors, along with staple items such as hair care and brushes, were displayed at the front for maximum exposure and attraction, while large, bulky items such as closet organizers were placed in back. The service counter cash wrap was put at the center of the space and surrounded by a variety of freestanding fixtures, also angled for maximum visibility. To display the merchandise to best advantage, all fixtures were custom designed. Several fixtures are on casters, enabling them to be used flexibly for seasonal and promotional purposes throughout the space, particularly near the open front entrance.

The interior uses white tile for floors and walls to achieve a clean image, complemented by light woods for a warm, homey look. The "wood" floor is actually vinyl, which saved considerable money while achieving an almost-real look. Primary colors—yellow, blue and red—were used for major accents and to promote a fun, festive look. The graphics, in keeping with that theme, use subtle neon call-outs for what might otherwise be named departments. Instead, the brushes department is "The Brush Bar," and mops and brooms are "Clean Sweep." Another design element is the house metaphor that shapes the store entrance and is found repeated in the trellis over the service counter-cash wrap. Also overhead, indirect fluorescent lighting reinforces the store plan, while movable incandescent spotlights and tracks are incorporated into the yellow overhead grid for added flexibility.

The Fuller Brush heritage was incorporated via backlit transparencies throughout the store that feature old photos of early products and tell the retailer's story in an entertaining, historical manner. The Brush Bar, the products upon which Fuller Brush built its reputation, is a museum-style display board featuring graphic information about each brush. The overall effect achieves a festive, powerful image.

Project: Fuller Brush
Location: Mesquite, TX
Client: Sara Lee Corp.
Design Firm: Retail Planning Associates, Columbus, OH

INTERIOR DESIGN TEAM:

Planner:	Brian Shafley
Designer:	Brian Shafley
Project Manager:	Paul Pizzini
Vice President in Charge:	Bill Sands
President/Chairman:	Bruce Krysiak
Lighting Consultant:	Larson Engineering
Merchandiser:	Barbara Engel
Graphic Designer:	Tim Bachman
Technician:	Craig Nowakowski
Photographer:	Robert Krusey

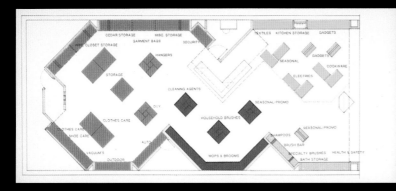

Floor plan

The house-shaped trellis over the service counter and cash wrap promote the "home" image.

Angled walls provide maximum visibility of merchandise from the mall.

Backlit transparencies promote the Fuller Brush heritage.

All fixtures were custom designed.

Primary colors—red, yellow and blue—provide a festive feeling.

J. C. Penney's "In Detail"

White Flint Mall, Bethesda, Maryland

HONORABLE MENTION, Hard Goods and/or Housewares Store Under 5,000 Square Feet

Designer: **Jacobs & Pratt, Inc.**

In Detail—an elongated space with a platform that doglegs deeper into the back of the store—provided a special planning and design challenge. Subtle design and decor changes now pull customers through the entire space.

The entrance sets the stage for the store's luxurious linens and accessories for bed and bath, with softly curved mahogany walls surrounding a patterned, Italian marble floor. Beyond this rotunda, the curved walls continue to pull the eye to the accessories window on the platform, which has a lighted-window treatment as its backdrop. From this point the perimeter cabinetry continues around the platform, inviting customers to sit at one of the design consultant's desks for the personalized shopping services.

One main objective of the design was to provide perimeter and freestanding flexibility for the various merchandise collections. The concept of a single category of merchandise in a specific location was not considered. Instead, binning, shelving and the ability to hang were kept "general" so that a collection in its entirety could be displayed on a segment of wall.

Complementary brass and wooden carts and gondolas were customized to provide presentation flexibility for the various merchandise collections.

The display points were punctuated with sparkle, via low-voltage lighting.

A patterned, Italian marble floor immediately sets an elegant tone.

Curved mahogany walls, floor-to-ceiling glass and a marble floor provide a grand "welcome."

Low-voltage lighting subtly and beautifully illuminates the bed and bath accessories.

Shelving had to be kept general so that
an entire collection of merchandise
could be displayed on a segment of wall.

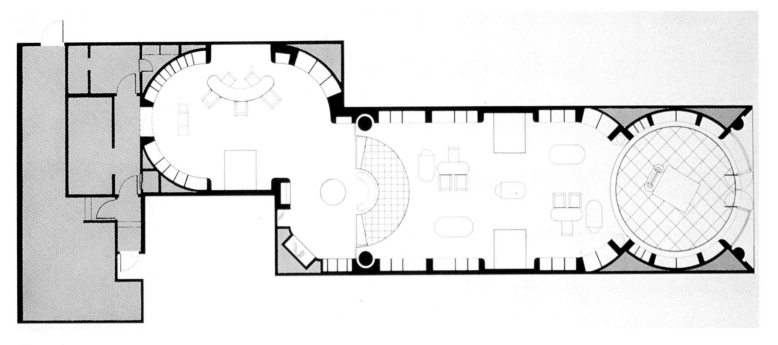

Floor plan

Customized brass and wooden
gondolas provide presentation flexibility
and sophistication.

INDEX